TRAINS AND COTTONWOOD SEEDS

POEMS BY LEANNA GASKINS

AN OLD LEOPARD (2015)

TRAINS AND COTTONWOOD SEEDS (2018)

Trains and Cottonwood Seeds

Poems by

Leanna Gaskins

Vinland Books

San Francisco ● *London*

International Standard Book Number: 978-1-7321785-1-9

Library of Congress Control Number: 2018903762

First published 2018 by
Vinland Books
2443 Fillmore Street
San Francisco, CA 94115

Vinland Books
27, Old Gloucester Street
London WC1N 3XX

www.vinlandbooks.com

1   3   5   7   9   10   8   6   4   2

In memory of my parents,

Ernest and Ruby Koehn

CONTENTS

✻

TRAINS AND COTTONWOOD SEEDS

I

Sitting in front of the depot,
Back from riding the train,
The air was filled with cottonwood seeds
And a peace that's hard to explain.
Something about the old depot,
The shining rails running by,
Distills a calm out of past years,
Lays a glamour over the eyes.
Yes, the people are hurried,
The day is bright and hot.
But this old place returns you
To times when they were not.
The blessing is in the freedom,
Those moments to stop and rest,
And let the trains do the running,
Ever again going west.
Knowing tomorrow will take you
Back to present time needs,
Precious the gift of sitting,
Watching trains and cottonwood seeds.

ALONG THE ROAD

II

Up across a far-off hill,
Gleaming in the early light,
A road slants silvery and pale.
Made mysterious by distance,
It climbs and dips and climbs again,
Both its beginning and its end lost,
Aligned to some strange star
That endows it with mystery.
Maybe it's just a road like this one.
But imagination layers it with images,
Visions of legend and experience,
And all unattainable longings.
It becomes a magical road
That imprisons the gaze
And sends us running
To retrieve our ruby slippers,
And go.

III

We'll get it figured out tomorrow,
For today's road was too long.
And we need a night of silence,
Before we can tell what is wrong.
We have run before the tempest,
And our bones ache with the stress.
What we missed while we were running,
Tonight we can only guess.
Give us this one night of silence,
Before we must answer make.
For the road has sapped our substance.
We have nothing left to stake.
When the gamble's on the table,
Give us time to read the take.

IV

Always rainbows seem fragile and fleeting,
Like soap bubbles that disappear at a touch.
But this one persisted,
Vivid along the edge of a cloud.
Not spanning the sky, but still
Showing all the colors bright and clear.
For miles along the road, it stayed,
Delighting the eye and the soul,
With this new lesson of creation.
The skies remain a place of wonder,
Where rainbows can endure and persist.

V

Like old lions, full of scars,
The tawny hills sleep beside the road.
Turning their weary backs to the sky,
They wait for what may come.
Long have they waited.
Years have eroded them.
Prey and enemies have scarred.
Now, somnolent, they scarce recall
Their fiery, tumultuous youth.
Enduring ice and rain,
Slowly subsiding, like all of us,
Under the accumulating burden of age.

VI

There is something about a road,
In the wideness of the west,
That beguiles the feet and the heart,
Calling, come and see what lies this way.
Dirt tracks, meandering across the red earth,
Gravel lanes, trending to the horizon,
Two-lane roads, whose distance is lost
Ever over the next hill,
Around the next curve.
Who can stay on the freeway,
When such songs call from everywhere?
Even if there's nothing more
Than more of the same,
There's something about a road.

VII

Well, yes, it was July,
But the mountain
Did not recognize the calendar,
And poured on us
A barrage of December.
In snow and bitter cold,
Up there along the crest,
Dressed for July, we shivered,
And fled before the artillery
Of snow and sleet and cold.
Down below the storm,
We found refuge
In more summery territory,
Where meadow and forest
Were more ready to accept
The dictates of the calendar page.

VIII

Like raindrops on a window,
The bubbles in the glass
Sparkle and seem to flow.
It rains beside me at the table
Where I sit and eat.
In the midst of loud music,
And bar chatter,
And silences—
Far from home at one more table.
Not my own or even friend or family,
Just a stop along the road.
But then,
Here they have raindrops
Beside the table.

IX

Sunshine loans, so read the sign
Beside the road, along my way.
And what a lovely thought it seemed,
To borrow sunshine for dark, gray days.
And maybe it's a bank as well,
To take sunshine deposits too.
Just think of equity you'd build
In sunny days all shining through.
The road is full of much surprise.
You never know what you may see.
But sunshine loans—a bright surmise
That traveled home from there with me.

X

What's it like out there,
In the stillness of the night?
On the road out there,
Where I cannot now stand,
All that way out there,
Where I've run in sun,
What's it like now when
All the sun is gone?
Here I sit quiet at home,
Gazing out at the night,
Wondering, what's it like out there,
Among rocks and hills?
Among stars and wind,
Do their shadows wait
For tomorrow's sun?

TIME AND CHANGE

XI

Well, here we are once more, my friends,
Beside the starting gate.
And all the bets are ranged against
The hope that we await.
Then shall we turn away in fear,
Just because they say,
We have no chance at all to be
Winners on this way?
You know their vision's limited.
They seldom clearly see,
Until the race has passed them by
In its entirety.
Oh, loudly they will howl us down,
And tell us to go home.
But we will run the course the same,
Winners when we come.
That last long stretch is just the one
Where we shall pull ahead,
And those who told us to go home
Shall slink away instead.

XII

Dusty rooms, piled full of old fables,
Sometimes the chambers of our life become.
Crowded with artifacts dull and corroded,
Darkened papyri, whose message is dumb.
Pallid the light through cobwebby windows,
Too pale to reflect in mirrors or glass.
Silent the wraiths of times gone and ended,
Leaving no mark in the dust as they pass.
Who can bring order into such chaos?
Where is the scavenger that we can pay?
To barge through the clutter, chase out the spiders,
And carry the useless detritus away.

XIII

We remember the old stories
That they used to tell us,
About the times, just a little while
Before we came there.
Just a turn away, and so
A little bit mysterious.
The things they said happened—
Somebody ran over
A rattlesnake in the road,
And its poison teeth were embedded
Somehow in the tire.
Then the driver was poisoned,
When he went to change it.
And lurid insects that inhabited
Gas station restrooms,
And the gym at school.
We never saw them,
And we thought it strange.
Yet we believed those old tales,
Left over from somewhere
Earlier than our time.
We tried with limited experience
To understand what they meant.
They're all gone now.
No vestige left of any of that.
Nobody thinks of snake fangs
Somehow embedded in today.

XIV

Change is the coin of living,
You early learn its way.
But nothing in your giving
Can mitigate the pain.
Change is full of detours
From every path you know,
And nothing gives you recourse
From what it overthrows.
Out of sunny morning,
You stumble into storm,
And nothing could prepare you
For what the day becomes.
Change will never warn you.
It just descends upon
The roads you thought were open,
And closes every one.
You think you have accepted
The changes you can see,
But far beyond your vision,
The changes multiply.
Oh yes, we think we've bargained,
And won the dark exchange.
But then the thing that matters
Is the thing we cannot change.

XV

The velvet curtains, I remember,
Heavy and dark, beside the stage.
A place of childhood, dim in distance,
That captured in folds of dark velvet
Childhood's lingering vision.
The tall, old building, I remember,
A room of dimness and people waiting,
Before the lighted stage,
Where my brief passage renewed
The image of velvet and age.
The railroad car, I remember,
A seat alone beside the window,
Going west forever,
Riding in the narrow space between
Velvet curtains and the sea.

XVI

How lightly we said it,
There's always next year.
And now that there isn't,
What can we say here?
Time passed and took with it
That foolish conceit,
Those things we did this year,
Would always repeat.
We forgot that the current
Of time is so swift.
It tears away moorings,
And casts you adrift.
Now what we let pass us,
That could have been done,
Is caught in that current,
Swept under and gone.
Oh, next year is coming,
Soon enough, it is here.
But for those postponed choices,
There is no next year.

XVII

Sometimes it comes to the place
Where you can't buy it any more.
Yes, you still have the money,
But now they've locked up the store.
They've now decided the items
You bought year upon year
Are no longer worth the selling,
So now they all disappear.
Isn't it true for all people,
The dreams of youth when we grow
Vanish in vapor of wishing,
Just when we think that we know
How to lay hold on the wishes
We couldn't possess years before.
Just when we lay down the dollar,
They rise and lock up the door.

XVIII

Wasn't that strange—
To find a remnant of the past,
When you were looking
For something else entirely.
Hidden among the embers
Of all the yesterdays,
There to suddenly appear
And spring to flame of remembrance.
What do they do,
These bits of our past lives?
How do they hide,
And then in sudden emergence
Appear and capture our delight?

XIX

And so the year is ending.
It was not a good year,
Full of many losses and sorrows.
And yet, we do not easily
Let go the old land,
And set sail upon the winter seas.
Reluctant we are, as in the twilight,
We lift the anchor and turn seaward.
The fires and fireworks burn on the headlands,
And folk dance carefree.
But here on the shore,
We lift our hands in prayer,
Before we lift the anchor,
And set sail into another year.

VISIONS AND FABLES

XX

Look how high their walls have risen.
Will they build across the sky?
What is this that they envision,
Rearing up their walls so high?
For a while it was just waiting,
Where the vast new structures rise.
There was silence among empty
Warehouse forms of lower size.
Old, sedate forms, now replaced
By the much more solid core
Of what we will have to live with,
When we see its final form.
Not unlike the Tower of Babel,
When it rose among the trees.
Shall we not also be frightened
At the form that stands where these
Old, flat-roofed, earth-toned dwellings
Served the needs of passers by,
Rather than a range of towers,
Trying to attack the sky.

XXI

The waters rush down through the canyons.
Yes, and with them they carry the canyons.
Stone by stone, building the rapids,
A tumble of years in the water.
The movement of time here stands visible,
For anyone with eyes that can see.
A curve in the crags lost suddenly,
Raw places where stones used to be.
And ever the water continues
Its perpetual dash to escape
The confines of canyons and chasms,
Ever changing the walls that it made.

XXII

ESCAPEES FROM GOMORRAH

We fled the city in the night,
With warnings we were told,
Without an understanding of
What future days might hold.
They said the dawn would not arrive,
Before the doom would fall.
And we must flee if we would live
Beyond the morning's call.
And so we found ourselves among
The empty fields at dawn.
And turning, looked to see what fate
Our city fell upon.
But gazing hard, we found that there
Was nothing left to see.
All we had known was lost and gone
In night's catastrophe.
So this the obligation borne
By those who came away,
To tell the tale that only we
Are granted leave to say.

XXIII

I would have sworn there was a wash
Of cold air coming down the hall,
When I emerged from hours of work,
And came to seek the night's recall.
From where it came was quite unknown,
For neither doors nor windows stood
Open to the night's cold wind,
To blow its mystery where it would.
Silent stood I, looking long
Past the doorways and the stair,
But the moment fled away,
With no hint of that night air.
Who can say from whence they come,
Visitations vaporous,
Coming on us unawares,
Leaving silence afterwards.

XXIV

Sloping down toward the great River,
The fields and gardens as we knew them,
Full of peace and all the power
That our kin could exercise then,
When we were the proud possessors
Of the Kingdoms of the River,
Where we thought the crown of being
Was bestowed, to last forever.
But somewhere mistakes undid us,
And the power drained away,
Till there's little left to speak of
What we were in our great day.
We heard tell that we offended
Some great god we did not know,
And for blasphemy, our leaders
Spoke, thus we are all brought low.
Sloping down toward the River,
Only deserts lie today.
Archaeologists inhabit
Palaces where kings held sway.
Only jackals howl in temples
Where our priests once stood to pray.

XXV

Starlight on the Great Green,
Mysterious and baleful.
The waters rock from sky to sky,
Dark with dread and terrible.
There is no moon to lend its light,
And make the sullen waters gleam.
The stars are far, their silver light
Just deepens mystery, it seems.
Some wind has roiled the ancient deeps,
And slanting waves crash everywhere.
The boundary of sea and shore
Has ceased to seem defined or clear.
The sea has bounds it may not pass,
So we are told, but in the night,
Fear asks, will the limits hold?
Should we turn now and take our flight?
Sea and shore are black with storm.
The stars await the star of day.
With dawn, the light transcends dark power,
And drives these ancient fears away.

XXVI

Well, that is what I thought I saw.
But then, my vision is never clear,
And all the street was full of mist,
Hard to see even what's near,
Let alone that uphill path
That might have held a wildcat's form.
And I will never know for sure
That what I thought I saw conformed
To anything you'd classify
As vision possible right here.
For this is just a city street,
And wildcats aren't known to appear
Among the condos and the shops.
And yet, it seemed I saw her spots,
That leopard who ignored what's known,
And walked along this street alone.
She is gone now, more or less,
And maybe won't be seen again.
But I will keep the picture clear,
Her walking there, cool and serene,
Walking there, in spite of all
The limits city laws install.

XXVII

We stand in a narrow place,
Like the one where the angel
Blocked Balaam.
And here between the rock walls,
Do we see the barricade?
Can we perceive the reason
Our passage is limited and dark?
It was not the road at fault,
Much less the transport,
When Balaam was stopped
At that narrow place.
Was it not perception,
Lack of vision, lack of grace?
Was it not reluctance
To recognize his time and space?
We think like him we're speakers
Whose words can have effect.
Perhaps we should be seekers,
And then we'd see the angel,
And know we should turn back.

XXVIII

November 11, 2011

It seems today's some kind of date,
Different from the surrounding ones.
And people thus commemorate
What has no meaning once it's done.
We try to mark the changing time,
And, taking note of months and days,
We foolishly imagine we
Can catch the flight of time's swift ways.
We seize on things we think to hold,
But find at last that, all the same,
It slips beyond our power to grasp,
And time's a beast we cannot tame.

XXIX

A petroglyph,
Ancient graffito.
And don't you wonder
Whether his mother said,
What do you think you're doing,
Writing on the wall like that?
Stark lines on red stone
Tell us so little.
Did the graffito writer
Get sent to sit in the corner?
Now when we look at them,
Can we even imagine
What inspired those lines,
Or the long effort it took
To inscribe them there?
Was it only a graffiti artist
Indulging his whim?
And did his mother
Box his ears for his insolent
Writing on the wall?

XXX

New moon tonight,
But there's no sky to see it.
Fog and darkness obscures
All our sight.
So we must listen
To hear the faint music,
The song of the new moon,
Just coming to light.
It's only hidden there,
Behind the fog's dimness,
Where it gleams in its newness,
Beginning its climb.
And if we but pause
To stand silent a little,
The song of the new moon
Will gladden our night.

XXXI

GOLD RUSH TWO

And then they found the gold in the prairie,
And after that, who cared it was our home.
They came from everywhere to get a piece of it,
And left us little to keep when they were done.
They clogged our streets with trucks and drill rigs,
And kept the roads impassable all day.
At night, they spilled their whisky in the clubrooms,
Their torrent washed our small town dreams away.
No place was left to live in peace and quiet.
The town was dragged along the downward slope,
Until we lost the very shape of our life,
Consumed in the hot fires of their hope.
It will come to nothing as they all do,
And boom will turn to bust and leave bereft
Alike the ones who came and wrecked our home town,
And us who find ourselves with little left.

VOICES

43

XXXII

Whispers, susurrous and strange,
Drift along the corridors,
Fill the house with vague unease,
Fading in and out of sense.
Here they lodge a little while,
Like a dandelion seed,
Caught aloft by fickle wind,
Then dropped among some rocky shoals,
With myriad little whispering pools,
Where the tide, in restless dance,
Back and forth among the stones,
Whispers secrets of the sea.
Always there's the undertow,
Currents of the hidden deep,
Voices that our ears can't know,
Unquiet vision out of sleep.

XXXIII

Hurry, hurry, say the voices.
Hurry, hurry, get it done.
Shall I bend myself to listen
To such cries that urge me on?
Shall I not instead deny them,
And take time to rest my soul?
For the building of my being
Demands more than running so.
In the silence of the morning,
Let me stand a while to wait,
Even if the day's requirements
Shout aloud beside the gate.
It's not they I need to answer,
It's not they I need to hear.
It's the Voice that speaks in silence,
Where in silence, life is near.

XXXIV

A leaflet advertising peace
Blew in underneath the gate.
I knew that it was only trash,
But the words caused me to wait,
And stop to read before I sent
That missive to the garbage pail,
Wondering if words' intent
Could ever in this way prevail.
Peace is a dream unknown, it seems,
And can't be reached by standard means.
So could a little paper's call
Come through where stronger efforts fall?

XXXV

Can you imagine what it would be like,
Hearing an angel's voice?
Do you think it would be delight,
A thing to make you rejoice?
These silly images we see portrayed,
Surely are far from what is real.
An angel stands in the Presence of God,
And sees what from us is concealed.
Such a being is awesome and bright,
With that incandescent flame,
No frail cupid or gossamer sprite,
But a majesty hard to name.
To hear an angel speak would be
To hear the clash of tectonic plates.
And seeing the face of an angel clear,
Like standing at the sun's furnace grates.
All unprepared for such radiant sights,
No wonder mortals cower in fear.
And none of us can imagine the sound,
What an angel's voice would be like to hear.

XXXVI

I closed my mouth upon the word
I thought and might have spoken there,
For it seemed better to lock up
That word and keep it unaware.
I closed my hand upon the blow
I thought and might have rendered then,
For it seemed well to wait a while,
And to rethink that blow again.
I closed my mind upon the thought
That rose and grew behind my eyes,
For it seemed best to suffocate
Such thoughts before they could arise.
Is not the world too full of this—
Of words and ways best left alone?
For there's no way you can recall
What once goes forth when it has gone.

XXXVII

Does it wind up like that?
Your name is maligned on Facebook.
Whatever your work or building,
Somebody hated you enough
To say you were a jerk and post
Its cruelty for the world to see.
When all the years are gone,
And what you said and did
Is written in the books forever,
Is that what it comes to—
That chat room trivialization,
Leaving your name encumbered
With hatreds you never even thought
Or imagined you might have inspired?
Once it was only kings and generals
Whose names were dragged
From past to present calumny.
Now who is immune?
How shall any of us escape
The petty amalgam of our time?

XXXVIII

I loved the word I heard last night,
Among the vanities and vain
Repetitions of the lies
And all the bitterness and pain.
I loved the word that breathed of truth,
Of sunlight shining among trees,
Where all the silly, sullen talk
Slid into silence and to peace.
I loved the joy of knowing just
A moment's quiet in the soul.
To be assured that such can be,
Among the terrors and the woe.
I loved the grace, oh Lord, you give,
Alone the refuge of the heart,
Beyond the limits of our lives,
That peace which you alone impart.

FAMILY ALBUM

XXXIX

The gulls fly low over the water,
Where gentle ripples pulse and sway,
With subtle hues of sunset light,
Reflected pinks and palest gold.
And rows of boats, at their mooring, dance
With glowing shadows over the bay.
Against the sunset, the great bridge stands
A fantasy of perfect curves,
And but for that, one could believe
We were back again on Puget Sound.
Back again in the lantern glow,
On the deck of a small and well-loved boat,
A cozy place where the family sat
To watch day end across the deep.
And soon with the dark to go below,
Drink a toast to a day a-sail,
Hearing the boats coming in to port,
Sailing past in the silent dark.
But those days are far away and gone.
The hands that raised a glass with us
Have crossed beyond the farther sea.
Yet here the harbor itself the link
Kindles the memory with sunset songs.
A touch as light as its slanting rays
Completes that circle among the rows
Of little boats rocking quiet at home.

XL

Did I learn it from you, Dad,
This long love of distance and roads?
Did I learn to hear the deep silence
That travels wherever we go?
Dad, I didn't know how to listen,
When you told about going to see
All the places you always would mention,
But they have made inroads in me.
I've gone to those places now, seeking
Understanding for what they could mean,
And I guess I'm arriving at meaning,
In remembering your old, spoken dreams.
Dad, I love the places you taught me,
Though you didn't know that you taught.
They're shrines on the road of my pilgrimage,
Milestones on the way that you sought,
And showed me without your intention,
Without my then knowing its name,
The road I must walk to its ending,
Unknown and still known all the same.

XLI

My mother made that for me,
I said, in a place long ago,
That my mother never would see.
And surprised I was to note
How strongly that spoke to the hearts
Of those young sophisticates,
Who saw Mom's beautiful way,
Her art with embroidery work.
It made them, hearing, to say
How perfect her work, and how they
Wished they could do work the same.
And more, how they wished they could say,
My mother made this for me.
Seeing her intricate work,
The stitches perfect and true,
They heard as clearly as I,
"My love made this for you."
And my life is written on this,
The good she helped me to see.
In heaven again I will say,
My mother made this for me.

XLII

CHRISTMAS EVE

We will not write the note tonight,
For they are gone, with whom we dreamed.
And now, the silence makes it hard
To keep a hold on what then seemed
Secure and certain, even though
We didn't really think the deer
Would eat the carrots that we left,
Or Santa drink our glass of cheer.
But now that we are left alone,
Tradition frays and little holds.
We hang the stockings, but we see
The past won't make it through the cold.

XLIII

LAST RUN

It was a drive like all the others,
Through the cemetery and the fields.
Looking at farms and little churches,
We talked of life in farming country.
Autumn had touched trees and bushes,
And we noted their bright colors.
There were sand plums still in ditches,
Where the children had not found them.
We laughed about their sourness,
And remembered when we sought them.
Mom smiled and tried to tell us
What she thought and still remembered.
Then we brought her back to supper,
And another silent evening.
One month later, we were driving
Out to that same cemetery,
To lay flowers on the headstone,
Where she lies beside our Dad.
We remembered in the sunlight,
How she said when last we brought her,
Looking at the stone and smiling,
"Ah, he was a good Dad."
And no one knew till then
That day had been
Her last run.

NEW EVERY MORNING

XLIV

An ordinary pot of clay,
Among the many in Your house—
So let me serve You all my days.
For there is room as well for those
Who have no power to shine like gold.
Then everyday tasks let me serve,
For there are many such, we're told.
And in my corner, let me stand,
While in this form I must abide.
For we clay pots are from Your hand,
As truly formed as silver bright.
And who can say what we will be,
When this our clay-form work is done?
Just let me be a faithful pot,
And I'll rejoice in what I am,
And in what You make me become.

XLV

Blind from birth, and sitting
There to beg his bread,
By the grace of God,
He met Christ instead.
When they questioned him,
They whose souls were blind,
He told them the truth
Which they could not find.
You say you do not know
How this thing can be.
I don't know the how,
But this I know, I see.
And the one you call sinner
Healed me with a word.
Whatever you may call him,
I call him holy Lord.
They rejected him,
But then, the Lord of Light
Came and welcomed him
With living inward sight.
Those who rejected him
So sure that they were right,
Also rejected the healing
That could have given them sight.

XLVI

I wish I owned the latitude
Where green, cool-shaded days
Await the weary traveler,
Who, long upon his way,
Comes with fortune's blessing bright
Into that cool, still port.
And there, to rest a day, a night,
In climes of gentler sort
Than all the hot, wind-blasted ways
We often find our lot.
Or bitter cold, benighted roads,
Where comfort there is not.
I wish I owned the longitude
Where mountains rise serene,
And all the dusk of valley fog
Is nowhere to be seen.
There where morning songs arise
Full hours sooner than
The darkling valleys, left in night,
Until the sun finds them.
But yet it is not ownership
My spirit most would hold.
It is the daily joy of sights
That are not bought and sold.
Just point me out the path to go,
Forget the owner's deed.
It is the glory of the place,
It is the joy you can't replace,
That truly we all need.

XLVII

Let's curl it around a finger,
That old strand of memory and dream,
That bright ribbon of sun and laughter.
Let's curl that around and keep
All that it means.
We'll curl it around our heart,
That strong strand of family and hope,
That broad weaving of time and growth.
We'll curl that around and hold
All that it gives.
We'll curl it around our living,
That golden strand of unity and grace,
That glowing chain of lives and loving.
We'll curl all that around and sing
The songs of all it means.

XLVIII

Name me the equation
By which to measure love,
By which to fathom faithfulness,
Or understand the depth and height
Where love abides and grows.
Name me too the square root,
The dividing power of hate,
By which the soul is driven out
And turned to devastation,
Where death alone prevails.
Then name me that pure total,
Where darkness is subtracted,
And light of love is multiplied,
To overturn all hate—
The everlasting perfect sum
Forever dark negates.

XLIX

GOOD FRIDAY

That day
Began in violence and tumult.
See them standing in the torch light,
Priests and elders, the Sanhedrin.
Can you see those other faces,
Full of Hell's own malevolence,
In the shadows there behind them?

That day
Went from travesty of trials
To an open declaration
That the innocent must suffer.
Justice utterly abandoned
In the clamor of the mob
And expedience of power.

That day
Fell to darkness at the noon hour.
Was it there behind the darkness,
Thick as nights among black rocks,
That the Father of the Lamb
Stood to see the sacrifice
Of the day of His atonement?

That day
There was mourning and lamenting
Among those who loved the Lover.
And the hand of God Himself
Tore the veil of the temple,

Just as humans, grieved at loss,
Tore their garments in their sorrow.

That day
Ended in a profound silence,
All the universe in sorrow
And confusion and unknowing.
Until the Third Day,
When the Word Himself, arising,
In the glory of His triumph,
Spoke redemption for all creatures.

L

The valley brims with light,
Rank on rank of golden river trees,
Lifting their flaming heads
To the perfect autumn sky,
Wild with those flying clouds.
Oh, glory of such a day!
How can the heart not rise,
Singing in praise and delight?
The hills themselves lift up,
Sweeping higher against the blue of sky.
The gold of the river of light
Is harvest of plenty to store up
Against the coming snows.

LI

Now, here we sit at the intersection,
Waiting for the light to change,
Impatient at the length of time
It takes to shift.
While over there,
On the cusp of the years,
The planets shift their feet in quiet,
Patient while the great revolutions
Finish their turn.
And somewhere far higher,
Starlight and galaxy-light stand,
Solemn before the throne of the All-Lord,
Bowed in stillness to wait.

LII

On this side, we can only see
A fraction of reality.
Our vision limited and dull,
We long to see the picture full.
On this side, we can only hear
The faintest echo of the clear,
Resounding hymn of endless praise
Which on that side will fill our days.
On this side, we can only touch
The slightest edge of holiness,
And reach with longing hearts to feel
The wondrous grace of its fulness.
On this side, we can only know
The faintest vision we are shown,
Until we come where all is clear,
And we shall know as we are known.

REVERIE AND REFLECTION

LIII

You come back to finish the task,
Thinking the pain will be hard,
To empty the house of its beauty,
Give away all the memories,
And even discard
The old chairs where you sat
To watch the sun set from the yard.

You come back to say your goodbyes,
And find it's already been done.
The people and places you knew
Are mostly half-faded,
Or fallen among
What no longer matters.
See, your heart is already gone.

You come back to finish the battle
That has burdened your heart for these years,
And find no traces of cannons,
Or even the landmarks
That inspired such fears.
Lost battlefield borders,
Where no sign or symbol appears.

LIV

The music curls like the leaf,
Like the flower petal, the song,
And listening is like knowing
Where all the beauty belongs.
The curve of the notes is like sunlight
Shining among the leaves,
And all the shimmer of voices
Echoes the glory it gives.
Here where we sit and listen,
The forest is far away.
But still, in the curve of the music,
We stand in its beautiful day.
If we be separated
By time and the sorrows we see,
Still, the curl of the music
Brings us back to the harmony.

LV

The old towels are frayed,
But I keep them,
Making room on the rack for them,
Among the useful and new.
A beautiful gift from a loved hand.
Too fragile to use;
Too precious to discard.
The old dreams are tarnished,
But I keep them,
Digging out the polish from time to time,
To smooth with careful hands
Their worn, old surfaces.
Too frail to use;
Too treasured to discard.
Among the pebbles and old jewelry,
In the boxes that will be dumped when I'm gone,
I keep them.

LVI

It isn't counted by the dollars
That they write next to your name.
It isn't counted by the titles
Or the honors they proclaim.
It isn't counted by the power
That some people hold so dear.
It isn't counted by the speeches,
Or the times that you appeared.
It's only counted by the numbers
Of the people that you taught,
And the legacy you gave them
In the knowledge that you brought.
It's only counted in the stories
That they'll tell and tell again.
It's only counted in the ledger
Filled with your long list of friends.

LVII

Lots of times, I do it the old way.
Yes, I know you can order it from Amazon.
But then, there is a kind of understanding
That comes from taking time
To look at things,
And see the form and texture.
Sure, you can just push the button,
And it will soon arrive,
Neatly packaged at your door.
But sometimes it seems clearer
To stand and look for a while,
And choose from all the vast
Array of choices, one
That really fits.

LVIII

Pain is my companion.
Like an old friend,
Who walks with you,
And speaks of things that sometimes
You'd rather not hear.
But you listen,
And try to understand the meaning.
It's like an old neighbor,
One you know and don't know,
And lean across the fence
To exchange complaints
About the neighborhood.
Coming and going,
Saying hello at unexpected moments,
And clinging to you at the corner,
To tell you stories you've heard
Too many times before.

LIX

Turn it upside down,
And empty the water
That collected in myriad droplets.
Drizzle descending,
Sky dropping,
Gathering there in pools.
Turn it upside down,
And empty the droplets
Of voices and visions.
What we all collect,
Gathering, glowing,
Into the pools of thought.
Turn it upside down,
And empty the depth
Of dream and longing,
All that builds with
The long, slow deposit,
The glitter and grit.
Turn it upside down,
And empty it
Into the vastness
Of evening and morning,
Moons waning and waxing,
And bottomless blue,
Where all the pools collect.

LX

You see them walking the dog,
With an expression of utmost uncaring.
Do they even think what passes
Through the mind of the creature
That walks there beside them?
Together, yes, but nowhere united.
And together, alone, walking
Among the passing sights—
Houses, trees, a fence, a gate—
For the one, comprehensible, if unnoticed,
For the other, remote, perhaps unapproachable.
Do they ever wonder what each other thinks?
Man and dog walking,
Together, but alone and separate,
Under a silent sky.

LXI

Back behind the edges of everything,
That's where the mountains begin.
But it's only outside our back door,
Only across the fence line,
That's where the mountains begin.
Look past the morning paper.
Look past the shopping list.
That's where the mountains begin.
Stand still and listen.
Stand still and wait.
That's where you'll hear the song.
That's where you'll see the gate.
That's where the mountains begin.

LXII

Because we walk down slowly,
Past all the stones and silence,
Where vestiges of yesterday
Are living in the rock.
Because the way is heavy,
Steep and full of obstacles,
We're forced to step so lightly
That we have time to look.
Because the rocks rise skyward,
Enclosing our steep pathway,
And all the walls are riven
With clefts and sundered stone,
Because the edges threaten,
And we must cling to those walls,
We have to look and listen
To what the cliff face tells.
Because there is no other
Way to make our passage,
We learn to walk in silence
And see the road we walk.
Because we walk down slowly,
Where haste would only hinder,
We learn to value slowness,
While still the learning holds.

LXIII

This is the border of home,
Like Pisgah, where Moses stood,
And beheld with longing the land,
Though come there he never could.
This is the border of home,
The haven for which we all seek,
Out here as we're walking alone,
Hoping the guide voice will speak,
Saying, this is the way to home;
This is the road, walk here.
Silence among the stones
Is most often the sound we hear.
But this is the border of home,
This the dream we embrace,
And struggle to find our way
Through wilderness to that place.
It seems almost within reach,
While still in distance we roam,
Walking here in the wilderness,
Along this, the border of home.

IMAGES

LXIV

Faded, old memories, frayed at the edges,
The legacy kept of years we have lived.
That is all gone now, just a few pictures,
A few dwindling stories are all we can give.
For the years and their content lie bundled together
In old dresser drawers and albums forgot.
Who will share now the old, hoarded memories?
There's little they'll see there but mildew and rot.
Sit down for a moment, and look at the pictures,
And think how it was when all things were new.
If no one who follows will care for our memories,
At least this is something for me and for you.

LXV

A burst of sunlight down the street,
As day is ending, floods with light
The houses and the boulevards,
Transforms them all to pure delight.
The power of the sunlight's gleam,
Among these ordinary streets,
Performs its magic so offhand,
We hardly know the dream it meets.
Thinking this the normal way,
With light-filled eyes, we go inland,
And soon see to our dark dismay,
No such bright gold lies there to hand.
Beloved is the sky and sea
That gives us this unfailing glow.
So blue, so gold, their glory gleams,
And nowhere else this gift to know.

LXVI

We dragged them with us from the past,
When we chose this life to make,
Those old vessels that we knew
Far too well then to forsake.
We dragged them with us, they protesting,
This was not their home to be.
But we brought them, and we used them,
In cherished continuity.
We dragged them with us, coming forward,
And they always do us good.
For we carried their grace with us,
Here from then, when still we could.

LXVII

Your faces in the pages of the paper
Arrest the gaze,
And make us ask,
Why have you come to such a pass?
You look like good and normal people.
Why have you fallen so,
And cannot justify
The deeds you surely thought
Would not ever be known?
Can you remember
What it was like to walk in peace?
When you never would fear
That your face would be shown
Among the cruel, the dark, the criminal?
Is it the sorrow to you that it should be?
And can you cry for grace,
From that front page?

LXVIII

The sky is empty,
And the city skyline has moved
Much closer.
It's strange and sad
To lose the old tree that stood there.
Sad to lose the tracery of branches
Against the sky.
That vision we knew for so long,
Now where shall our gaze go?
There is just blankness there,
And all the rustle of leaf and branch
Is gone.
The birds are gone too,
Along with the dappled shade.
It is a void,
A cold and sorry loss,
Only a common sort of tree,
But it was beautiful against the sky.

LXIX

It was the town of legend,
But it was just where we lived.
They made the movies claiming
To portray its wilder past—
Dirt streets and longhorn cattle—
But it was just streets and alleys,
Where we grew up alone.
We didn't know the history,
Beyond the bits and pieces
We picked up on the days when
They all rode by on horses,
And staged the showy gunfights.
It was the town of legend,
But we were just the children
Who grew up in the shadows
Of cowboys and the stampede
Of time closing off
Whatever those old days were.
So when the day came calling,
To ask us who we would be,
We didn't know the legend.
We thought it was pretending.
And so we left the memory,
To find our way alone,
To build up our own legends,
Far from where we'd grown.

LXX

Pretty girl on the catalog cover,
You look so bemused,
As if you wonder how it happened
That you find yourself there.
You're new to us, not seen before,
With your gentle, happy face.
Maybe it's all new to you too.
So bright and young,
Sweet to see your curving smile
And unpretentious delight,
That tilt of the head that says,
"Can this be me?"

LXXI

A little brown snake on the railroad track,
Warming himself in the sun.
Well, he was alright this time.
It was a quiet track,
With no trains until evening.
But so fragile a thing,
Staking his life on a chance
Of escaping those steel wheels,
Just to lie in the sun for a while.

A little green snake on the pathway,
Where I almost stepped on him.
Unknowing, he lay in the sun.
He could not have imagined
How fragile his life,
With heedless human feet,
And bicycles rushing along.

Poor little creatures,
So brief their lives,
Condemned to so deep a need
For the sun and warmth
We casually take for granted.

STONES

LXXII

Into the wild rock lands,
The road has led today.
Horizon to horizon they stand,
Rough and regal against the sky.
Folded, striated, broken,
Pinnacles red or golden,
Ramparts and battlements unscalable.
Among them, the road darts fitful,
Curving and weaving to find a path,
Struggling up and plunging down.
Vistas sometimes open afar,
With layer on layer of mesas and cliffs,
Rising to mountainous heights.
Often they frown on our passage,
And signs warn of rocks flung
From their brazen tops.
Small are we in these places,
The road a narrow trail,
Passage granted for only the moment.
Here, the wild rocks rule.

LXXIII

Like Jacob, I made the rock my pillow.
For the way was too long,
And the frowning cliff too high,
For my feeble steps to go on.
So to lie down in silence among stones
Is better than silken sheets,
When all the soul bows down in pain,
And stark weariness seeks sleep.
Yes, and who can say of stones
That they may not become
The staircase leading past the cliff,
Where darkness is undone.

LXXIV

The smooth, calm contours
Of a turquoise stone
On the necklace under my hand,
Is remembrance of cliffs and canyons,
And a little mining town,
Where they still keep those
Tangible memories of grace.
Touching the stone's gentle curve,
Remembering that cool day,
And the sure and sudden knowledge
This piece of sky and dream
Was mine to hold.

LXXV

A sequined rock caught the morning sun,
Up along the river.
It gleamed in splendor.
And oh, don't you wish
You could wear such beauty?
Subtly golden and sewn with silver paillettes
That catch the sun
And splinter it a thousand ways.
Ah, but take heed.
It would be dull if you tore it
From its native hillside.
Without the sun,
It would be lost,
And you most likely
Would not even see it.

LXXVI

The dark shape of the cliff
Will inhabit my night.
So grand and still it stands,
In sunshine and in indigo silence.
I know its rough surfaces well.
For days now, I've wakened to see
How morning light transformed its dark bulk.
And now, turning to sleep,
It's comfort to see
How its calm, brooding form
Looks down in peace.

OLD RIVER

LXXVII

Old river, you're stupendous today,
Running bank to bank,
Far wilder and darker
Than ever before I've seen you.
Your waves pour over the rocks,
And lap around the roots of the trees.
Tree limb and tree trunk ride your crest,
And doubtless, down below,
Even the river rocks roll and tumble
At the will of your currents.
The canyon walls echo
To your joyous springtime shouts,
And the rafters are nervous,
As well they should be.
Your hidden traps remain,
And your cold waters fill them with danger.
No wonder they built the railroad
As high as they could above your tumult.
Ah, your placid summer face beguiles,
But now, wild river,
We see you true—
Your power and fierceness
Unheeding and unchallenged.

LXXVIII

Some of the time, old river,
The sound of you fades from memory.
Once the miles pass between us,
Your voice loses intensity.
Memory holds you lightly,
But memory holds you long.
Faded the sound of your singing,
But lingering the voice of your song.
Some of the time, old river,
In the early dawn, I awake,
Thinking I heard you laughing
Up there by Hanging Lake.
When I'm away, old river,
Maybe sometimes you're a dream.
But most of the time, I think you're
Far more real than daylight can seem.

LXXIX

Ah, patient old river,
Depleted, deprived of your water,
Left gaunt and sadly weakened,
Seekers and rafters forsake you.
Lone and silent you wait,
Accepting loss, ignored.
You rock between your banks,
And gently smooth the stones
You lately tossed and battered,
Without rancor, calmly,
Your steady course unchanging.
Where the rocks stand naked now,
Soon no one will see them.
It is but a brief season—
Just a still eddy—
And your memory is long.

LXXX

Old river, I wish I had time
To study your moods and your changes.
I wish I could sit on your bank,
And watch the seasons pass.
I'd like to see the reflections
Of clouds and lightning,
Of moonlight and starlight,
On your bright water.
I wish I could wait
For the silence of snowfall,
And the first birdsong of spring.
Old river, I know I could learn
A lot about life from you.
If only I had the time
To sit and listen and watch.
But I am a transient creature,
Not flowing on always like you.
My days are too short for your measure,
And I must settle for what little,
What short little times I can do.

LXXXI

A quiet morning, bright and cool,
And you, old river, are full of your own sparkle,
Though turbulent and dark underneath.
The leaves are turning,
And the canyon shadows brood.
But you, shining and grand,
Romp between the impassible cliffs,
Singing your old song,
The chant you sang when once,
Eons ago, they say,
You ran up there where cliff tops soar,
Just beginning to sculpt their sheer, astonishing walls.

SEASONS OF THE RAILROAD

LXXXII

Here beside the railroad,
Where all the dreams went west,
Standing here in silence,
Wondering at the changes,
We find here less and less.
Our dreams went west with the railroad.
Our dreams went west and stayed.
Now when we stand by this railroad,
Now when we stand looking westward,
Our hearts are all dismayed.
It was night here on the railroad,
When we rode by going west.
Everything passed unseen then,
All was lost behind us,
Going away on our quest.
Now in the sun by the railroad,
Seeing what didn't count then,
Wishing we'd known what was missing,
Wishing we'd cared just a little,
Now that it won't come again.
Here now beside the railroad,
Where no one still dreams today,
Seeing that life all went westward,
Seeing that change is forever,
We find nothing left here to say.

LXXXIII

Little pink roses there on the hillside,
Blooming among the rocks and weeds.
You'd wonder why, if you didn't know
A town stood there upon that slope.
Above the railroad, little houses,
Where people cared enough for beauty
To plant those sturdy pink roses.
And now, when all else is gone,
Even the massive railroad structures,
Briefly yet, though lone and starving,
Those little roses stand their ground.

LXXXIV

The few remaining images
Of things we used to know
Line the walls along the streets,
Where now nobody goes.
The railroad tracks meander through
The vacant, dim-lit streets,
Where nothing moves along the rails
But rats and wind-blown weeds.
And light itself seems distant here,
Where shadows crowd the walls,
And all the ghosts of yesteryear
Have left for brighter halls.
These silent, solemn bricks that saw
The commerce build the town,
See only dust and cobwebs now,
And wreckers tearing down
What's left of once proud legacies,
We frittered all away.
Their fanciful, old memories
Won't make it to the day
When all this vast accomplishment,
Now given a new name,
Shall shine in tawdry luster
That has forgot the flame.
That power burnt out long ago,
The day the railroad went.
Now these are only forlorn streets
Whose fortune is all spent.

LXXXV

The brakeman walks along the line,
And throws the switch for one last time.
The engine and the cars roll through,
And nothing more is left to do,
But close the switch and walk away.
And thus the Alder Branch died today.
Alder Town will scarcely miss
The trains they casually dismissed.
But farmers down the line will see
A shocking rise in transport fees.
And then the elevator too
Will wither from lost revenue.
The town itself will shrink and say,
What could have brought us down this way?
And who will realize the lack,
When they tear up the branch line track?
It was the life of Alder Town,
With it the town's life too goes down.

LXXXVI

In here all is dead and still,
Trophy heads and empty bones,
Even if they picture well
The glory of a time that's gone.
Like bones of dinosaurs, they stand,
Their life long lost to those who come
To gaze a bit in wonderment,
Take a picture, and move on.
They moved the nation yesterday.
Our fathers loved their power and grace.
The fading remnants of that love
Bring their grandchildren to this place.
But just outside museum walls,
The living railroad still runs by,
Shaking walls and drowning talk,
With its long-known, thrilling cry.
Look now through that window there,
Just beyond the old caboose.
The offspring of these trophies runs,
The living railroad on the loose.

INDEX OF TITLES AND FIRST LINES

ABOUT THE AUTHOR

LEANNA GASKINS spent her early years on a Kansas wheat farm without electricity, gas, or inside plumbing. She went to school in Dodge City and then to the University of Kansas, transferring when invited to a program in economics at Rampart College, in the mountains of Colorado.

She moved to Los Angeles where she spent several years and married. She graduated as a Regents Scholar from the University of California, Berkeley, and earned a Ph.D. in Linguistics there, applying modern formal linguistic theory to the ancient Egyptian language written in hieroglyphic, which she also taught to a generation of UC Berkeley Egyptology students.

Anticipating the coming importance of personal computers, she moved to Silicon Valley to join very early startup software companies as a teacher, writer, and manager of writing groups. During this same period she researched railroad history in travels over all the western states, and was one of a small team who rebuilt and restored the long-dormant Southern Pacific 2472 steam locomotive.

She retired very early and moved with her husband to central London where they lived and studied for ten years, after which they returned to live in San Francisco. She has written poetry since her early college years.